Socks

Connie Knight

Tellwell Talent
www.tellwell.ca

ISBN
978-0-2288-2940-9 (Hardcover)
978-0-2288-2939-3 (Paperback)
978-0-2288-3311-6 (eBook)

DEDICATION

To my daughters Olimpia, Candice and Sabrina who filled me with love, enchantment, fulfilment and a truly Magical life.

To my husband David for your love, support and putting up with my countless ideas and giving me my step children David Rhys and Jessica who have completed my family with joy.

ACKNOWLEDGEMENTS

To my sister Carol Manuele who edited my books and your support you have given me, I am so grateful.

Thank you to Tellwell publishing for making the journey of my books come to life

Green socks,
Blue socks,

Yellow socks,
New socks.

Socks with holes,
Socks with bows,

Socks with stripes
On its toes.

Socks
with aeroplanes,
Socks with a train,

Socks with ducks
in the rain.

Socks
with teddy bears,
Socks with cakes,

Socks
with pretty lace
that mumma makes

Socks with boxes,
Socks with cats,

Socks
with all different
coloured hats.

Socks with flowers,
Socks with gates,

Socks with pink dotted plates.

Socks
with cherries,
Socks with a wish,

Socks
with my favourite
Little fish.

BIBLIOGRAPHY

Connie Knight has been a hairdresser for 40 years. During these years she has dabbled in Footwear, Hat and Bag making and currently has a home registered kitchen making desserts and cakes for functions.

Connie has written 7 children books when her 3 daughters Olimpia, Candice and Sabrina were very young while being a sole parent. Watching the girls play, inspired by their magical world of make believe, ideas started flowing and the first book Socks was born. She is currently releasing her 7 books the first being socks and has started to write again, back to her love of creating an imaginary world of adventures and learning for children.